D1543749

From a
GRANDMOTHER'S
HEART

MEMORIES *for my* GRANDCHILD

BY RUTH O'NEIL

CASTLE POINT BOOKS
NEW YORK

www.stmartins.com

www.castlepointbooks.com

The Castle Point Books trademark is owned by Castle Point Publications, LLC.

Castle Point books are published and distributed by St. Martin's Press.

Designed by Tara Long

Illustrations used with permission from Shutterstock.com

ISBN 978-1-250-16364-6 (hardcover)

Our books may be purchased in bulk for promotional, educational, or business use.

Please contact your local bookseller or the Macmillan Corporate and Premium Sales Department
at 1-800-221-7945, extension 5442, or by e-mail at MacmillanSpecialMarkets@macmillan.com.

First Edition: March 2018

10 9 8 7 6 5 4 3 2 1

Contents

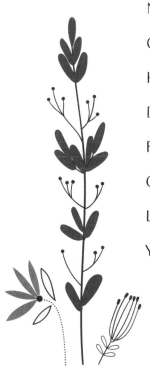

INTRODUCTION

Some of the greatest stories are those passed down from generation to generation. It's time to pass your story down to those you love most. This journal will guide you and inspire you as you reveal your best and most notable memories and take pause to consider the people and events in your life that helped make you who you are today.

You'll find plenty of space to jot down all of the interesting details that you want your grandchildren to remember about you and generations past. Fill in the answers and tell the story of your life, one valuable piece at a time.

This journal is as much a delight for you as it is for your grandchildren. Enjoy completing the pages of this book and revisiting the past before offering this heartfelt gift to your grandchild to treasure for the rest of his or her life.

Childhood

MY BIRTHDAY

DATE: TIME:

....

AS A BABY, I WAS:

....

....

HERE'S A PHOTO OF ME AS A BABY:

THE STORY BEHIND MY NAME

[*My full name at birth:*]

HOW OR WHY MY NAME WAS CHOSEN:

....

....

NICKNAMES I'VE HAD SINCE:

....

....

THIS IS HOW I FEEL ABOUT MY NAME:

....

....

....

....

ON THE DAY I WAS BORN...

THE PRESIDENT AT THAT TIME:

....

POPULAR ENTERTAINERS AT THAT TIME:

....

....

....

....

POPULAR FASHIONS AT THE TIME:

....

....

....

The #1 song:

....

....

....

WHERE I GREW UP

MY ADDRESS:

....

HERE'S A PICTURE OF MY CHILDHOOD HOME:

MY FAVORITE MEMORY OF THIS HOME:

....

....

WHERE I CAME FROM

COUNTRIES MY ANCESTORS CAME FROM INCLUDE:

....

....

....

THIS IS WHAT I KNOW ABOUT MY ANCESTORS (AND YOURS!):

....

....

....

....

I CELEBRATE MY ANCESTRY BY:

....

....

....

FRIENDS

{ *My best friend as a child:* }

....

....

THINGS MY FRIEND AND I WOULD DO TOGETHER:

....

....

....

ONE STORY ABOUT A CHILDHOOD FRIEND:

....

....

....

....

....

MEMORIES FROM MY CHILDHOOD

MY FAVORITE TOY OR ACTIVITY AS A CHILD:

....

....

....

MY FAVORITE BOOKS AS A CHILD:

....

....

....

....

MY FAVORITE SHOWS OR MOVIES:

....

....

....

....

GAMES I PLAYED:

....

....

....

Family and friends who took care of me:

....

....

....

MY EARLIEST MEMORY OF CHILDHOOD:

....

....

....

....

MY SCHOOLS

THE NAME OF MY PRIMARY SCHOOL:

....

THE NAME OF MY JUNIOR HIGH:

....

THE NAME OF MY HIGH SCHOOL:

....

My grades in school were:

EXCELLENT   AVERAGE   POOR

ONE THING I LIKED ABOUT SCHOOL:

....

....

....

....

ONE THING I DIDN'T LIKE ABOUT SCHOOL:

....

....

....

My best subject:

....

MY WORST OR LEAST
FAVORITE SUBJECT:

....

....

....

....

ONE AWARD OR HONOR I GOT IN SCHOOL:

....

....

....

....

....

....

ONE TIME I GOT IN TROUBLE AT SCHOOL:

....

....

....

....

....

....

....

MY MOST INSPIRING TEACHERS

[*Best elementary school teacher:*]

HERE'S WHY:

....

....

[*Best middle school teacher:*]

HERE'S WHY:

....

....

[*Best high school teacher:*]

HERE'S WHY:

....

....

ADOLESCENCE

AS A TEENAGER, I WAS...

....

....

....

MY RESPONSIBILITIES INCLUDED...

....

....

I WAS EXCITED ABOUT THINGS LIKE...

....

....

I WORRIED ABOUT...

....

....

MY MENTORS

THE PEOPLE I LOOKED UP TO AS A KID:

....

....

THIS IS WHY I LOOKED UP TO THEM:

....

....

*This is one lesson
I learned as an adolescent:*

....

....

THIS IS ONE THING I HAD TO FIGURE OUT LATER:

....

....

My Family

My Family Tree

Love your family...
Make no room for regrets.
Tomorrow is not promised
& today is short.

—Unknown

MY MOM

THIS IS WHAT I'D LIKE TO TELL YOU ABOUT MY MOM:

....

....

....

....

THIS IS WHAT MY MOM LOOKED LIKE:

....

....

....

JOBS OR HOBBIES MY MOM HAD:

....

....

....

THE FUNNIEST MEMORY I HAVE OF MY MOM:

....

....

THE FONDEST MEMORY I HAVE OF MY MOM:

....

....

....

HERE'S A PHOTO OF MY MOM:

MY DAD

THIS IS WHAT I'D LIKE TO TELL YOU ABOUT MY DAD:

....

....

....

THIS IS WHAT MY DAD LOOKED LIKE:

....

....

This is how my parents met:

....

JOBS OR HOBBIES MY DAD HAD:

....

....

THE FUNNIEST MEMORY I HAVE OF MY DAD:

....

....

THE FONDEST MEMORY I HAVE OF MY DAD:

....

....

....

HERE'S A PHOTO OF MY DAD:

MY SIBLINGS

THIS IS WHAT I'D LIKE YOU TO KNOW ABOUT MY SIBLINGS:

....

....

....

....

....

HERE'S A PHOTO OF MY SIBLING/SIBLINGS:

HERE ARE THE NAMES OF MY SISTERS AND BROTHERS
AND A LITTLE INFO ABOUT EACH:

[   ]

....

....

[   ]

....

....

[   ]

....

....

[   ]

....

....

[   ]

....

....

MY COUSINS

THE COUSINS I KNOW BEST ON MY MOM'S SIDE:

....

....

....

....

....

{ *Cousins are those childhood playmates who grow up to be forever friends.*
—Unknown }

MY COUSINS I KNOW BEST ON MY DAD'S SIDE:

....

....

....

....

....

HERE IS A FUN MEMORY OF
SPENDING TIME WITH COUSINS:

....

....

....

....

....

....

HERE'S A PHOTO OF MY COUSINS:

MY GRANDPARENTS

HERE'S WHAT I'D LIKE YOU TO KNOW ABOUT MY GRANDPARENTS:

....

....

....

....

MY GRANDPARENTS' PROFESSIONS:

....

....

....

....

HERE'S AN INTERESTING STORY ABOUT THEM:

....

....

....

....

STORIES ABOUT MY FAMILY

FAMOUS PEOPLE WE'RE RELATED TO:

....

....

....

Family: where life begins & love never ends.
—Unknown

ONE FAMILY LEGEND:

....

....

....

ONE SECRET ABOUT MY FAMILY:

....

....

....

FAMILY TRADITIONS

SOMETHING MY FAMILY DID IN THE SPRING:

....

....

....

....

SOMETHING MY FAMILY DID IN THE SUMMER:

....

....

....

....

SOMETHING MY FAMILY DID IN THE FALL:

....

....

....

....

SOMETHING MY FAMILY DID IN THE WINTER:

....

....

....

....

My favorite holiday tradition:

....

....

....

ONE TRADITION I'D LOVE FOR YOU TO CONTINUE:

....

....

....

....

....

BIRTHDAYS THEN AND NOW

HOW I CELEBRATED BIRTHDAYS AS A KID:

....

....

....

HOW I PREFER TO CELEBRATE MY BIRTHDAY NOW:

....

....

....

A BIRTHDAY GIFT THAT WAS SPECIAL TO ME:

....

....

....

MY FAVORITE BIRTHDAY MEMORY

[*I remember the day I turned* ....]
AGE

THIS IS HOW I CELEBRATED:

....

....

....

....

....

THIS BIRTHDAY WAS MEMORABLE BECAUSE...

....

....

....

....

....

....

MILESTONES

AGE WHEN I LEARNED TO WALK:

....

AGE WHEN I LEARNED TO SWIM:

....

Age when I learned to ride a bike:

....

AGE WHEN I LEARNED TO DRIVE:

....

CELEBRATING WITH FAMILY

THE HOLIDAY THAT I LOVED MOST AS A CHILD:

....

ON THIS DAY, I WOULD:

....

....

....

My favorite holiday now:

HERE'S WHY:

....

....

....

....

NEW YEAR'S EVE

The best New Year's Eve I can remember:

WHERE I CELEBRATED:

....

....

....

WHO I CELEBRATED WITH:

....

....

....

....

....

HALLOWEEN

AS A KID, I WOULD DO THIS ON HALLOWEEN:

....

....

....

....

THE BEST HALLOWEEN I EVER HAD:

....

....

....

....

NOW THAT I'M A GRANDMOTHER, THIS IS
WHAT I LIKE ABOUT HALLOWEEN:

....

....

....

THE 4TH OF JULY

HERE'S WHAT I DID AS A KID ON THE 4TH OF JULY:

....

....

....

MY FAVORITE 4TH OF JULY MEMORY:

....

....

....

....

HERE'S HOW I LIKE TO SPEND THE 4TH OF JULY NOW:

....

....

....

THANKSGIVING

HOW I CELEBRATED THANKSGIVING AS A KID:

....

....

WHO WAS THERE:

....

....

FOOD WE ALWAYS ATE:

....

....

WHAT WE DID BEFORE OR AFTER EATING:

....

....

HOW I LIKE TO CELEBRATE IT NOW:

....

....

HOLIDAY TRADITIONS

MY FAVORITE HOLIDAY TRADITION TO SHARE WITH YOU:

....

....

ONE HOLIDAY I COULD DO WITHOUT:

....

HERE'S A PHOTO OF ME SPENDING THE HOLIDAYS WITH FAMILY/FRIENDS:

During My Lifetime

HISTORIC MOMENTS FROM MY CHILDHOOD

MEMORABLE NEWS FROM MY CHILDHOOD:

....

....

....

....

How we got the news:

....

....

A HISTORIC DAY I'LL NEVER FORGET:

....

....

....

....

....

HISTORIC EVENTS IN MY ADULTHOOD

HERE'S A NEWSPAPER CLIPPING FROM A HISTORIC DAY IN MY LIFE:

THIS IS HOW I FEEL ABOUT THAT EVENT NOW:

....

....

....

NEWEST FADS WHEN I WAS A TEENAGER

CLOTHING:

....

....

....

....

CARS:

Slang Words

....

....

....

....

....

FADS I JOINED IN ON:

....

....

....

....

....

WHEN I GREW UP I WANTED TO BE...

MY DREAM PROFESSION AS A KID:

....

....

....

....

OTHER JOBS I CONSIDERED OR TRIED:

....

....

....

MY CAREER TURNED OUT TO BE:

....

....

....

....

MY FIRST JOB

NAME OF THE COMPANY:

....

JOB TITLE:

....

Do not follow where the path may lead.
Go, instead, where there is no path
and leave a trail.
-Ralph Waldo Emerson

HERE'S HOW I GOT THE JOB:

....

....

....

....

HERE'S HOW I FELT ABOUT MY FIRST JOB:

....

....

....

....

....

....

....

....

THIS IS WHAT I LEARNED FROM IT:

....

....

....

....

....

....

PROUD MOMENTS

ACADEMIC ACHIEVEMENTS:

....

....

PERSONAL ACHIEVEMENTS:

....

....

....

PROFESSIONAL ACHIEVEMENTS:

....

....

Honors or awards I earned:

....

....

I FELT REALLY PROUD OF MYSELF WHEN I...

....

....

....

....

MY FAMILY WAS PROUD OF ME WHEN I...

....

....

....

....

I'M PROUD OF YOU BECAUSE...

....

....

....

....

PLACES I'VE VISITED

VACATIONS I TOOK CLOSE TO HOME:

....

....

....

....

*One place I wish
I could travel to:*

VACATIONS I TOOK A LITTLE
FARTHER FROM HOME:

....

....

....

THIS IS MY FAVORITE PLACE TO VISIT AND WHY:

....

....

....

HERE'S A VACATION PHOTO OF ME:

LOCATION OF PHOTO:

....

APPROXIMATE DATE OF PHOTO:

....

A PLACE I'D LIKE TO SHOW YOU:

....

....

....

PROGRESS

I NEVER THOUGHT I'D LIVE TO SEE:

....

....

....

....

....

....

An invention I couldn't live without:

SOMETHING THAT I HOPE WILL HAPPEN IN MY LIFETIME:

....

....

....

....

....

Favorites

SOME OF MY FAVORITE THINGS
TO DO AS A CHILD

THINGS I ENJOYED DOING INDOORS FOR FUN:

....

....

....

THINGS I ENJOYED DOING OUTDOORS FOR FUN:

....

....

....

HERE'S SOMETHING I LOVED DOING WITH MY FAMILY:

....

....

....

SOME OF MY FAVORITE THINGS
TO DO AS AN ADULT

THINGS I ENJOY DOING INDOORS FOR FUN:

....

....

....

THINGS I ENJOY DOING OUTDOORS FOR FUN:

....

....

....

HERE'S SOMETHING I STILL LOVE DOING WITH MY FAMILY:

....

....

....

....

MY FAVORITE MUSIC AND SONGS

A SONG THAT BRINGS BACK MEMORIES:

....

THIS IS THE MEMORY IT INSPIRES:

....

[*My favorite singer now:*]

THE TYPE OF MUSIC I ENJOY NOW:

....

....

CONCERTS OR PERFORMANCES I ENJOYED IN MY LIFETIME:

....

....

....

....

MY FAVORITE RECIPES

MY FAVORITE MEAL TO MAKE:

....

MY FAVORITE DESSERT TO MAKE:

....

A TRADITIONAL MEAL IN OUR FAMILY:

....

I'D LIKE TO TEACH YOU TO MAKE:

....

....

....

....

Here is a recipe I'd like to pass down to you:

....

Ingredients: Directions:

....
....
....
....
....
....
....
....
....
....

Here is a recipe I'd like to pass down to you:

....

Ingredients:

....

....

....

....

....

....

....

....

....

....

Directions:

....

....

....

....

....

....

....

....

....

....

....

MORE FAVORITES

FAVORITE COLOR:

....

FAVORITE FOOD:

....

FAVORITE ANIMAL:

....

FAVORITE PASTIME:

....

FAVORITE KEEPSAKE:

....

MY FAVORITE THING ABOUT
BEING YOUR GRANDMOTHER:

....

....

....

....

....

....

....

Getting to Know Me Better

MY HABITS

GOOD HABITS:

....

....

BAD HABITS:

....

....

HABITS I'D LIKE TO START:

....

....

HABITS YOU SHOULD AVOID:

....

....

CHARACTER TRAITS

MY BEST CHARACTER TRAITS:

....

....

MY WORST CHARACTER TRAITS:

....

....

HOW PEOPLE THINK OF ME:

....

....

HOW I SEE MYSELF:

....

....

....

A DECISION I WAS GLAD I MADE

The best decision I made:

....

....

....

WHAT HAPPENED AS A RESULT:

....

....

....

MY ADVICE TO YOU WHEN YOU MAKE A BIG DECISION:

....

....

....

....

A DECISION I REGRETTED MAKING

THE WORST DECISION I MADE:

....

....

....

WHAT HAPPENED AS A RESULT:

....

....

....

MY ADVICE TO HELP YOU HAVE FEWER REGRETS:

....

....

....

....

....

DEFINING MOMENTS IN MY LIFE

A PERSON WHO MADE A BIG DIFFERENCE IN MY LIFE:

....

....

....

[*Here's how he/she made a difference:*]

....

....

....

HERE'S HOW YOU HAVE MADE A DIFFERENCE IN MY LIFE:

....

....

....

....

....

MY DREAMS AND GOALS

DREAMS AND GOALS I HAD AS A CHILD:

....

....

....

....

HERE'S HOW THOSE DREAMS TURNED OUT:

....

....

....

DREAMS I HAVE FOR YOUR FUTURE:

....

....

....

....

RELIGION

MY RELIGIOUS AFFILIATION:

....

....

THE ROLE RELIGION PLAYED IN MY CHILDHOOD:

....

....

THE ROLE RELIGION PLAYS IN MY LIFE NOW:

....

....

....

....

....

....

THE PEOPLE AND EVENTS THAT SHAPED MY BELIEFS:

....

....

....

....

....

....

....

HOW MY BELIEFS DEFINE ME:

....

....

....

....

....

....

....

I HAVE ALWAYS BELIEVED:

....

....

....

I have complete faith in...

....

....

....

HERE ARE SOME OF THE BELIEFS AND VALUES
THAT I'D LIKE YOU TO GROW UP WITH:

....

....

....

....

....

....

DATING

HERE'S HOW I MET YOUR GRANDFATHER:

....

....

....

OUR FIRST DATE:

....

....

....

....

....

OUR AGES AT THE TIME WE MET:

Him: Me:

....

MY FIRST IMPRESSION OF HIM:

....

....

....

....

*A nickname
I call him:*

....

....

....

....

SOMETHING INTERESTING ABOUT HIM:

....

....

....

....

....

....

THIS IS ONE OF MY FAVORITE PHOTOS OF US TOGETHER:

A FUNNY STORY ABOUT HIM:

....

....

....

....

....

....

ABOUT YOUR GRANDFATHER

YOUR GRANDFATHER'S ANCESTRY:

....

....

HIS PROFESSION:

....

THINGS HE ENJOYED DOING:

....

....

....

....

....

....

....

....

What made me fall in love with him:

....

....

....

WHEN YOU WERE BORN, YOUR GRANDFATHER...

....

....

....

HERE IS WHAT YOUR GRANDFATHER
LOVES MOST ABOUT YOU:

....

....

....

....

....

OUR WEDDING

PLACE: DATE:

....

Maid of Honor:

....

Best Man:

....

ON THE DAY OF MY WEDDING, I...

....

....

....

....

....

....

A MEMORABLE MOMENT FROM MY WEDDING:

....

....

....

....

....

....

HERE'S A PHOTO FROM MY WEDDING:

CHILDREN

THE NAMES AND BIRTHDAYS OF ALL MY CHILDREN:

....

....

....

....

....

THIS IS HOW I'D DESCRIBE YOUR MOM/DAD AS A BABY:

....

....

....

....

My age when I had your mom/dad:

....

....

THIS IS HOW I'D DESCRIBE YOUR MOM/DAD AS A CHILD:

....

....

....

....

WHY I'M PROUD OF YOUR MOM/DAD:

....

....

....

....

SOMETHING ELSE YOU PROBABLY NEVER
KNEW ABOUT YOUR MOM/DAD:

....

....

....

....

OUR FAVORITE THINGS TO DO TOGETHER

WHAT I ENJOY DOING WITH YOU:

....

....

....

WHERE I LIKE TO GO WITH YOU:

....

....

....

I'LL NEVER FORGET THE DAY THAT WE...

....

....

....

IT MAKES ME SO HAPPY WHEN YOU...

....

....

HERE'S A PICTURE OF THE TWO OF US:

SOMETHING I'D LIKE TO DO WITH YOU SOMEDAY:

....

....

....

....

....

....

HOW WE ARE ALIKE

APPEARANCE:

....

....

CHARACTER TRAITS:

....

....

Likes:

....

....

....

Dislikes:

....

....

....

THINGS YOU DO THAT REMIND ME OF ME:

....

....

MY HOPES FOR YOU

WHAT I WANT YOU TO ATTAIN IN LIFE:

....

....

EDUCATION

....

....

CAREER

....

....

LOVE

....

....

FAMILY

....

....

DREAM BIG

ADVICE FOR MAKING YOUR DREAMS COME TRUE:

....

....

ADVICE FOR DEALING WITH ADVERSITY:

....

....

WHY YOU SHOULD FOLLOW YOUR DREAMS
WITH ALL YOUR HEART:

....

....

*I hope your dreams take you to the corners
of your smiles, to the highest of your hopes,
to the windows of your opportunities, and to the most
special places your heart has ever known.*
—Unknown

FROM MY HEART TO YOURS

WHAT I WANT YOU TO LEARN FROM ME:

....

....

WHAT I WANT YOU TO REMEMBER
ABOUT WHERE YOU CAME FROM:

....

....

NEVER FORGET THAT I...

....

....

MY LOVE FOR YOU IS...

....

....